THE TEN CINEMAS OF C

This booklet outlines the development of cinem
relation to their impact on the Buckinghamshire t
has moved from the first small, flickering, black and white pictures of the 1890's
to the current wide screen, colour and sound shows and the story of Chesham's ten
cinemas reflects this on the changing nature of the films, audiences and cinemas.

Chesham was well placed to embrace the cinema. It was then one of the larger
towns in the County with a strong industrial and agricultural base and had access
to the railway. The first films were shown as scientific marvels and as such were
exploited by extrovert travelling showmen. One visited a fair in Chesham's
Broadway in 1900 and then this led to films being shown in existing halls, until
the first purpose-built cinema was opened in 1912. Responding to the increasing
sophistication and popularity of films, this was matched by a succession of ever
better cinemas – culminating in the art-deco magnificence of the Embassy in 1937.

With the last war, attendances reached a peak, but with the subsequent onslaught
of television, by 1982 the Embassy was demolished to make way for flats. Soon
only about 10% of the cinemas in the UK were left, but gradually there has been a
resurgence of attendances due to better quality films and presentation. In Chesham
this was matched by the showing of films at the original Elgiva theatre and now by
its successor, which is fully equipped to present films to professional standards.

The booklet finishes with the likely impact of the latest technologies, such as 3D,
and the increasing use of digital electronics.

Colour illustrations: Inside front cover and on the rear cover:-
Post-war views of The Embassy Cinema, Chesham. (Alan Body Collection)

First Published May 2010

2nd Edition August 2010

By: Clive Foxell,
4 Meades Lane,
Chesham,
Buckinghamshire   HP5 1ND
(clive.foxell@btinternet.com)

ISBN 978-0-9564178-0-0

Printed by: Orbitpress Ltd.,
11 Market Square,
Chesham,
Buckinghamshire. HP5 1HG

THE TEN CINEMAS
OF CHESHAM

Dr Clive Foxell CBE FREng

PREFACE

Various experiences led to my interest in the cinema and now this book. As a boy, like most of my generation, a major influence was the pleasurable ritual of going to the cinema, as well as the content of the films. In the 1930s and 40s, the cinema represented a place of comfort, warmth, social contact and the possibility of luxuries such as an ice cream, whilst the films themselves, in general, portrayed a way of life that most could only aspire to. By comparison with the theatre and the radio, it was then the most sought after form of entertainment and much of the media was filled with news and gossip about the film world. In those days, few had cars, had flown or had travelled to any extent, but the cinema made places like Los Angeles (or 'LA') seem quite familiar. It is therefore hardly surprising that the cinema was a tremendous influence on people of my generation.

As a teenager I became attracted to science and engineering and so I became more interested in the technical aspects of photography and film making. This was given a boost when I joined the GEC Research Laboratories as an apprentice and found that one of my first projects was working with Technicolor to introduce a new GEC light source (the compact source lamp) that was intended to provide the extremely high light levels then required for Technicolor filming. As this was at the end of the Second World War, there was only one of the complex Technicolor cameras in this country so, as the equivalent of a 'tea boy', I was privileged to visit most of the studios and see many of the 'stars' and film-makers of that time. Being on the sets of films such as 'Scott of the Antarctic' and seeing people like that doyen of cameramen, Jack Cardiff, in action were memorable experiences and gave me a considerable insight into the realities of filming. Equally, I sometimes had to project the test films that had been shot in order to demonstrate the advantages of our new lamp and this also gave me experience of operating professional 35mm projectors. Being at a time when some of the original (and highly inflammable) nitrate film stock was still in use, this could be a traumatic experience.

In 1956, my wife and I were married in Chesham and have lived there ever since, thus witnessing the decline of the local cinemas under the onslaught of television, to the current renaissance. In 1999 I arranged a display in Chesham Library on the history of the local cinemas for the Chesham Town Museum Project. Since then, I have discovered much more on the subject and given numerous lectures and written articles. This booklet is a summation of this work, intended to put on record the story of the cinemas of Chesham and set it in the wider context of the evolution of the film industry.

Clive Foxell   Spring 2010

CONTENTS

ACKOWLEDGEMENTS

I am deeply indebted to Ray East for many of the illustrations used in this booklet. Others are from my own collection, of which some are 'orphan' works, where the origins and ownership are uncertain. In these cases, whilst diligent searches have been made to determine their true ownership, I apologise if any of the attributions are incorrect.

My thanks are also due to the staff of Chesham Library and of the Bucks Local Studies Centre at Aylesbury for their assistance. I would also like to acknowledge the contributions I have received from local people, such as Peggy Wilson, the late daughter of Charles Wilson, the owner of the first purpose-built cinema in Chesham, Dave James for his recollections of the children's Saturday morning shows and also the many others who knew the cinemas well.

CAF

INTRODUCTION

It may seem surprising that Chesham could have had ten cinemas – even although not all at the same time! Probably this view comes from thinking of Chesham as a small place in a rural setting, and somewhat behind the times. After all it did not get a railway until 1889, but by then Chesham had become a significant Bucks town with a population of some 6,500. It was the centre of many small agriculture-related industries employing a large number of skilled artisans and craftsmen. Indeed when the railway did eventually arrive in 1889, these augmented the commuters and (with the aid of cheap workmen's tickets) began to work in London.

So Chesham was certainly large enough to attract early cinemas and with the continual improvements in films and their presentation it was not unusual for the cinemas to evolve in the manner described in this book. In the early days this was partly due to the fragmented nature of the film industry and research suggests that the evolution of Chesham's cinemas is probably typical of a number of towns of similar size. The criterion I have used for inclusion in this list of cinemas are that they were commercial shows for the public, but of course there were many other ad hoc screenings.

THE PIONEERS

In a sense, the first moving pictures were centuries ago when people discovered that these could be created by a hand casting shadows from a fire or lamp onto a convenient surface. This led to complex shadow puppet shows, which are still very popular in the Far East. Later, when the Jesuits developed a crude projector using an oil lamp and lens in 1626, this became the basis of the 'magic lantern' which could show still pictures, and with the advent of brighter pictures from the 'limelight', it became very popular by the mid 19th century. Professional 'lanternists' now came to give shows in Chesham and elsewhere using hand-coloured and complex moving multiple slides - complete with a musical accompaniment. One of the most popular of these featured 'The Battle of Waterloo'!

For a long time it had been realised that apparent movement could be recreated by using a property of the eye called 'persistence of vision'. For, if the eye briefly sees a picture, it is held by the brain for rather longer. Thus a series of such still pictures (- usually at a rate of more than 16 per second) can

By the mid-19th century the 'magic lantern' had become very popular and so professional 'lanternists' used great ingenuity in improving their shows by using multiple slides and other techniques to create the illusion of movement. This led to the development of the cinema. (Clive Foxell Collection)

merge to create the impression of movement. Optical toys were produced which allowed a person to view a sequence of drawings through a slot in a rotating drum, in effect producing a simple cartoon film. With the discovery of photography by Fox-Talbot in 1840, instruments like the Zeotrope could provide a brief moving picture for a single viewer and these evolved into the 'what the butler saw' machines usually found at the seaside. However the images could only be watched by one person.

All the practical techniques for producing moving pictures became available a roughly the same time. Most nations have made claims to have invented the cinema. In America, Edison threw a considerable team at the problem, then vigorously patented their work and commercially exploited it via his 'Bioscope'. The Lumiére brothers in France developed a process that was closest to what we would now recognise as the cinema. Whilst in this country, William Friese Green is often hailed as the inventor, but it is currently believed that probably the first was a man from Yorkshire, Louis Le Prince who made a basic cine camera and took a sequence in the main street of Leeds in 1888. Strangely, he then disappeared whilst visiting Paris to patent his invention.

Although many claim to have invented the cinema, it is now thought that it was Louis Le Prince, a Frenchman living in Leeds, who achieved it in 1888. This shows some of the images he took of the High Street in Leeds with his camera using paper negatives. His strange disappearance so soon afterwards remains a mystery. (Clive Foxell Collection)

However at that time photographs could only be recorded on paper which was a considerable limitation to projecting the image, and it needed the subsequent invention by George Eastman (who founded Kodak) in 1889 of a clear nitrate film base which could carry a photographic image which enabled not only the modern cine camera to be realised, but also a practical projector to show the film. Both depended on an intermittent mechanism that held the film steady during filming or projection and then moved it rapidly forward for the next frame. Of course these cameras and projectors were operated by hand 'cranking', the films were just 'black and white', without any sound, and stories were explained by means of titles spliced into the films.

These pioneers initially hired halls to show scientific and other learned societies their brief films in order to prove the veracity of their inventions. These first films usually consisted of scenes of exotic places and fauna, views from moving trains and simple incidents. It is difficult to imagine the impact that watching films for the first time had on the audience, who would try to pull the screen away believing that there really was a train there! Recognising the tremendous potential popularity of such demonstrations, magicians and travelling fairground showmen sought to incorporate films into their shows.

Typical of those touring shows to visit Chesham, was **'Professor' Alf Ball** – such prefixes as 'Sir', 'Lord' and 'Colonel' were added to give a suitable aura of authority to their shows. As a champion prize fighter, Ball started with a travelling boxing show, added more attractions and then a Bioscope. He came to the charter fair in the Broadway around 1900, with a traction engine 'Alfred the Great' (for haulage and generating electricity) pulling a 'caravan' (which acted as living quarters and unfolded to create a large black tent for the cinema). This caravan also had a small stage for the 'parade-ers' – performers who drummed-up customers - and alongside would be a magnificent Gavioli barrel organ to provide a musical accompaniment for them. The artistes were Madame Paulina (a funny lady midget), two dancing girls and Mlle Olga (a daring trapeze artist). The show consisted of short films of the view from the front of a moving tram, a fire brigade, workers leaving a biscuit factory at Reading, a train collision and some trick photography. Unfortunately, Ball was forced to give up after a series of unusual accidents to his show, including a fire caused by sparks from the engine - damage whilst on a train - jack-knifing whilst going downhill - and a lightning strike! Discouraged, he went back to just touring with a 'galloper' (roundabout), but his son married Mlle Olga!

Around this time the educational opportunities for films were recognised by schools and religious bodies who sponsored shows in a number of Chesham's churches. These subjects developed into significant activities and in later years were the reason that J. Arthur Rank entered the film business.

Travelling showmen like 'Professor' Alf Ball below, used the 'Bioscope' as an attraction and he visited Chesham around 1900. The traction engine (right) provided the power; the caravans became the entrance with 'parade-ers' to attract the customers and an organ (left) provided the music. Films were shown in a black tent at the rear. (Tommy Green)

The Rink Electric Picture Palace in Red Lion Street (on the site now occupied by The Water Meadow Surgery), looking towards the original Red Lion Public House. Itinerant Bioscope operators showed short films there in 1905. (Ray East Collection)

From 1907, the original Town Hall in Market Square occasionally began to show films and these proved so popular that regular performances began in 1912. (Ray East Collection)

THE 'SILENT' ERA

Next, in 1905, travelling Bioscope operators showed films at the Roller Skating Rink in Red Lion Street. Re-named **The Rink Electric Picture Palace,** films were then shown on a regular basis. These films were still quite short, but were beginning to tell a story. In 1907 the original **Town Hall** in Market Square started to show films occasionally and opened regularly as a cinema in 1912. The first British story film, entitled *'Rescued by Rover'* made by Cecil Hepworth in Hove was very popular and soon 'wild west' films began to arrive from America. These films were accompanied by a pianist, Mr E Culverhouse. There would be three performances on Saturdays, with seats at 2d, 4d and 6d. However it was soon to be eclipsed by a new specially built cinema.

The invention of the principles of moving films had led to a variety of different incompatible processes in making and showing films. But their popularity and rapid exploitation forced the acceptance of agreed techniques and standards based on 35mm film for professional work. Thus by the early 1900s the fundamental format of cine cameras and projectors had been established, but these were capable of incorporating tremendous technical evolution over the years to add sound, colour and many other features.

Illustrating the evolution of cine cameras: A photo taken on the set of 'Scott of the Antarctic' in 1948 showing the early hand-cranked camera used by Henry Ponting on the original 1910 expedition, in comparison with the modern Technicolor camera (in its sound-proof blimp) with the Director of Photography, Jack Cardiff. (Ealing Studios)

But the main thrust of cinema exploitation continued to come from fairground entrepreneurs. Indeed, Chesham's first purpose-built cinema was created by Charles Wilson, in 1912, at the top of Station Road. He was another showman, with his previous addresses ranging from England and Ireland to Iceland, and occupations from dry cleaner, haulage contractor to motor trader! He was persuaded by friends Messrs Gabriel and Wickes to create a cinema at Tonbridge in Kent and then built a number, including at Tring, Watford and Berkhamsted. **'The Empire'** in Chesham was built by Rust & Radcliffe of steel and concrete with an auditorium of 60' x 40' and some 400 seats set on a sloping floor for better viewing. As the then films were highly inflammable, the projection room was an isolated 'glasshouse' built over the entrance porch and much emphasis was placed on the fireproofing of the building and the number of fire exits. On the 4th July, the show that opened the cinema was similar to that earlier of Alf Ball, but the films were now rather longer and accompanied by a Henry Rose on the piano. With seats at 2d, 3d, 4d and 6d, the charity opening with '*Saved by Her Lion*' raised £4–15s for Chesham Cottage Hospital. However, following the tradition of the earlier 'parade-ers', there were still live performers on the stage, typically – 'Lady Little' who was 25" tall and '*a meteoric success in 5 continents*'! Wilson travelled weekly to Wardour Street in London to choose personally the films to be shown. After the introduction of the first newsreels he sometimes even shot his own films of local sporting events. The Empire was a great success, boosted by the consequences of the First World War and possibly the availability of double seats at the rear of the cinema!

In the centre, a rare picture of the new Empire Cinema in Station Road. Viewed from Dungrove Farm, looking towards the new houses being built in Stanley Avenue. (above and opposite Clive Foxell Collection)

The Empire Cinema opened on the 4th July 1912 and used the latest Kamm projector.

As all the films were silent, titles were used to explain the story. Initially most films were British, such as the very popular 'Rescued by Rover' made by Cecil Hepworth.

During the First War American pictures, such as Charlie Chaplin comedies, began to dominate. Newsreels were first introduced in to the programme around 1911.

The Empire continued showing silent films, which were now becoming of 'feature length' with well-known stars. Such films had to be supplied on several reels and required two projectors to show them, so that smooth changeovers could be made between reels. Expert projectionists could make this change in a 'seamless' manner that was not noticed by the audience. Business declined after the war and the Empire closed as a cinema in 1920, when Wilson hired it out for functions until the Second World War when it was used as a billet for troops. After the War, it continued to be used for events, such as Chittenden's annual radio and TV show, but then it became a packing depot of Van Houten's until an office block was built on the site.

After closure as a cinema, the Empire Hall became a popular venue for social functions. Under the heading, 'Lancashire lass tickles local coppers', *this shows Gracie Fields entertaining the local police force at their annual dinner.* (CAF Collection.)

Chittenden's, the local electrical retailers held their own 'Radio Olympia' each autumn in the Empire Hall. Usually it was opened by a local personality: in this case Margareta Scott, the film actress. (Clive Foxell Collection)

To cope with the growing demand in 1914 Charles Wilson built another cinema nearby – the **Chesham Palace**. It was on the site now occupied by Superdrug in The Broadway and had 505 seats, with a stage plus two dressing rooms for performers and a foyer flanked on each side by Brandon's display windows. The cinema opened on 26 June showing *'Neath the Lion's Paw'*, with seats at 2d to 1/-. The silent films were accompanied on the piano by a Mr Rose or a Mrs Stillman who rehearsed with the new films on the Monday mornings. There was an ex-guardsman as a formidable commissionaire to control the long queues and boys from Dr Banardo's sold the chocolates. At the time of the 'flu pandemic, as a precaution, the usherettes sprayed the audience with disinfectant. In 1922, Charles Wilson again used a cine camera, this time to film a Chesham v Slough football match with the intention of showing it at The Palace. Although he took the precaution of arranging to have the film shown at Slough, in case they won, fortunately Chesham won 5-1!

Built by Charles Wilson to respond to the growing popularity of film-going, the Chesham Palace opened on 26 June 1914. This picture taken in the early 1920s of one of the many celebrations held in the Broadway, shows how the entrance to the cinema was surrounded by two of Brandon's display windows. (Ray East Collection)

A study of the programmes at the Empire and Palace cinemas during this silent era reveals the evolution of film production. Initially, a typical show would consist of a series of short films interspersed by live performers. The latter were gradually phased out as the films grew longer and 'stars' began to emerge. Typical of such items on the Chesham screens featured a *'Lieutenant Pimple,'* in such comedies as *'Lieut. Pimple and the Missing Submarine'.* This

CHESHAM PALACE

Broadway, Chesham.

General Manager — H. Barr.
Resident Manager: W. Dunham.

June 15th, and During the Week, Continuous Performance

MONDAY, TUESDAY, & WEDNESDAY	BILLY & RED MAN
THE	FACE of FEAR
ENCHANTRESS	SKELLY BUYS HOTEL
	LIEUT. PIMPLE & THE
A Splendid Drama in 2 parts.	STOLEN SUBMARINE
THURSDAY, FRIDAY & SATURDAY	BUNNY'S MISTAKE
	INVISIBLE HANDS
BABY SPY	OH WHAT A NIGHT
A Selig Masterpiece.	Dupin & Sammy in a Side-car

PRICES : 3d., 6d., & 1s.

CHILDREN'S MATINEE:

Special Programme on Saturday at 2.30. Prices: 1d., 2d., & 3d.

A typical early programme for the Chesham Palace now with fewer, but longer films.

Whilst a few British pictures still featured, such as the Fred Evans series on 'Lieut. Pimple' (left and see poster above), the big box-office successes tended to be major American productions like 'Ben Hur' starring Fred Niblo (right). (CAF Collection)

main character was a music hall performer, Fred Evans who, with his family made a long running series of parodies of British attitudes, using a studio on Eel Pie Island. Starting in a similar small way, performers like Charlie Chaplin, Mary Pickford and Douglas Fairbanks Snr - and their films - became famous.

So by the mid 1920s the popularity of the silent cinema had grown to an extent which began significantly to change the structure of the industry. In the early days, people like Charles Wilson could build a cinema in Chesham and

18

go up to Wardour Street by train to choose the films to show the next week from a host of small independent film makers. But by now, audiences expected the films to be longer and more ambitious i.e. *Ben Hur* and *The Big Parade* which led to a greater prominence of the 'stars', growth of larger studios and grouping of the cinemas to obtain greater market share of audiences.

THE COMING OF SOUND

Having achieved moving pictures, the pioneers now turned their attention to providing colour, sound and 3-D films. Whilst the advertising for the Empire sometimes proudly proclaimed films in colour, in reality these were made by individually tinting by hand with a paint brush each frame of the film of about 80,000 frames! Although Pathé achieved some passable results, it was impractical on a large scale and acceptable colour films had to await the later development of Technicolor.

After many unsuccessful attempts to introduce a sound system using synchronised recordings, in 1928 the film 'The Jazz Singer' was launched to great acclaim based on such a disc system. However, it was soon replaced by an integrated sound on film processes. (Clive Foxell Collection)

The first sound films were shown in 1928, but this was only by means of a gramophone record synchronised (hopefully) with some parts of the film. With the arrival of proper sound actually recorded on the film, Wilson closed the Palace in 1930 for re-equipment with the latest Western Electric sound system and re-opened it as **The Astoria**.

19

Wilson converted The Palace to show sound films (which were recorded in synchronism on the film) in 1930, and reopened it as The Astoria. (Ray East Coll.)

Although this prospered, Wilson realised soon that a new wave of super cinemas were being built by the larger 'chains' of exhibitors, and the role of the small independents was limited, so he leased The Astoria to Shipman & King. In retirement, he lived at a house he had built in Eskdale Avenue in Chesham and, as a cricket enthusiast, often entertained Don Bradman and the visiting Australian Test team. Shipman & King also provided him with free tickets for his old cinema. In the face of competition from other cinemas it finally closed on 23 May 1959, becoming a Co-operative Society furniture shop.

The entrance to The Astoria in 1960, awaiting its redevelopment. (Ray East Coll.)

VERTICAL INTEGRATION

The coming of sound, and the investment required, encouraged further rationalisation of the film industry. Studios grew larger and began to take control of other aspects of the business, particularly distribution and exhibition, in order to become more powerful. They put numbers of popular actors under contract, made films on a production line basis and bought up chains of cinemas to ensure that their films were shown and that they thus got a reasonable return on their considerable investment.

The first of this new generation of more spacious and luxurious cinemas destined for Chesham was intended to be **The Regal,** situated in The Broadway on the site previously occupied by the local Co-operative Society when it moved to the Upper High Street.

The Regal would have been one of the new generation of imposing modern cinemas in Chesham, where the old Co-Op would have been cleared to enable it to be set back from the road and to allow a large car park at the rear. (Clive Foxell Collection)

For in 1935, Pathé, through Union Cinemas, announced the construction of this 1,000 seat cinema with 'a rustic brick front in keeping with the old traditions of Chesham'. However, the asking price for the site was too high and caused them to abandon the project and so it was left to Shipman & King to add another cinema to their existing circuit by building a new cinema in Germain Street in 1937. They already owned about 36 cinemas in the outskirts of London which tended to show the new films rather later than in the Greater London area. The cost of hiring films was related to the initially high cost of the prints and, as they became worn with use, they became cheaper to hire. Equally, a chain like S&K would reduce costs by passing the same film daily between nearby cinemas (i.e. The Embassy, Chesham: The Regent, Amersham: The Rex, Berkhamsted), usually by the boy projectionist on a bicycle!

Although S&K already operated The Astoria in Chesham, they were also looking for a suitable site to build one of the new generation of larger cinemas.

The Faithorn House in Germain Street, looking towards Town Bridge, with a sign announcing the imminent arrival of The Embassy cinema. (Ray East Collection)

After the negotiation for the ex-Co-op site fell through, they turned to a site in Germain Street. This had been occupied by the daughter of Dr Faithorn (a notable local personage) and her loyal companion Miss Potter. The S&K **Embassy** was quickly designed by David Nye in striking Art Deco style and is now regarded as a classic of that time. However, it now seems as if many of the most striking internal decorative features were the work of a Michael Eagan. Built by Bovis in just 19 weeks, it was air-conditioned and initially seated 1,146 people (reducing to 1,098 over the years), with provision for an organ, although one was never installed. The circle was supported by a 72ft x 5ft 6in girder, which had been transported by rail to Chesham Station and then hauled through the town at midnight, in order to avoid disruption. The cinema formed the centre of an impressive block containing flats and shops, enhanced by neon lighting. The striking foyer created the impression of entering something special for a pleasing experience and was surrounded by staircases leading to the circle and a stylish glass and chrome café. It was opened on 11 January 1935 by Cllr E. Culverhouse (CUDC Chairman, who had originally played the

22

The 72ft long girder to support the circle of the new Embassy was brought by rail to Chesham station and thence by a powerful LNER tractor, via Market Square, to Germain St.. It was done at midnight in order to avoid disruption. Bovis completed the construction of the cinema in just 5months. (Ray East Collection.)

After the formal opening, the week continued with 'Everybody Dance' with Jack Hulbert & Cicely Courtnedge. The cinema manager would soon occupy one of the flats and Marshall's open a car showroom below. (Ray East Collection)

The spacious auditorium of The Embassy cinema initially held some 1146 people, where the stalls were at 3 prices and the circle seats at 2 prices. The projection ports can be seen behind the circle and the whole raked to give good visibility of the screen. (Ray East Coll.)

The art-deco styling of designers Nye and Egan culminated in the magnificent café with its chrome and glass fittings, complementary carpets and lighting. It offered a fine view over Germain St. and was entered from stairs at the circle level. (Ray East Coll.)

The impressive foyer, shortly after completion, and before all the 'lobby cards' and advertisements for films such as –' now showing', 'next week' and 'coming shortly' - covered the walls. Behind the central ticket kiosk lies the confectionery counter and on either side grand staircases lead to the circle and café. (Ray East Collection)

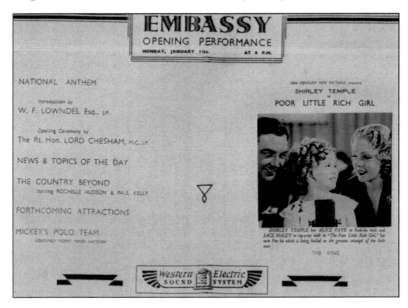

The special souvenir programme for the formal opening of The Embassy on the 11 January 1937. Unfortunately, both the scheduled main speakers became ill and it fell to Cllr. E Culverhouse, Chairman of the Chesham Urban District Council to deputise.

piano for the silent films shown in the Town Hall!), as Lord Chesham and Squire Lowndes were both ill. However, adding some glitz to the occasion, John Loder the film star, came in make-up straight from Elstree Studios in his role as Bulldog Drummond. The opening films were Shirley Temple in *'Poor Little Rich Girl'* and a Mickey Mouse cartoon. For the rest of the week the film showing became *'Everybody Dance'* with Jack Hulbert and Cicely Courtnege.

The souvenir programme - and a poor picture of the actor, John Loder, being welcomed.

By this time the growth of cinema attendances had driven the industry to a further level of rationalisation. After years of research, Technicolor had finally perfected a satisfactory colour film process which, albeit expensive, launched the era of 'blockbusters' such as *'Snow White' and 'Gone With the Wind'*. Soon the phrase *Glorious Technicolor* became part of our language. To make such expensive films on a regular basis, the studios merged into larger vertically integrated operations and this in turn favoured the major cinema circuits (Odeon, ABC, Granada etc) that were to dominate film presentation.

The introduction of the Technicolor process was a key factor in the success of the cartoon 'Snow White and the Seven Dwarfs' *and then* 'Gone with the Wind'. (Clive Foxell Coll.)

The cinema became the most popular form of entertainment with a twice-weekly change of programme and - where shown - an older film on Sunday. Inevitably, there had been controversy over the question of opening on a Sunday, with strong objections from some of the local churches and support from others. Bucks County Council did not allow Sunday performances until 1947, however for those who wished to see a film, they could always take a bus to the Rex at Berkhamsted over the border in Hertfordshire!

The Embassy closed for safety reasons with the outbreak of war in 1939, but soon reopened to maintain morale. The owners, S&K, were bombed out of their London offices and moved into the Embassy café and flats. But in 1940, four bombs straddled Germain Street, killing an evacuee, who had tried to escape from London, in Gooding's Forge and damaging the frontage of the cinema. There is a relevant episode of the popular TV series *'Dad's Army'* which shows the Home Guard platoon entering the Embassy.

Obviously, a post-war picture of The Embassy cinema, but still showing to the left the bombed-out premises of Goodings Forge and the blast-damaged windows of the hairdressing and betting shops to the side of the Cinema entrance. (Ray East Coll.)

THE WARTIME EXPERIENCE

After the initial closures for safety concerns, the War brought a further surge in cinema attendances. On one hand, the growing privations and lack of relaxation motivated people to seek the only form of entertainment readily available, in addition the Government realised that films were an ideal way of widely disseminating information and propaganda to boost morale. A consequence of this understanding and the shortage of films lead to the resurgence of the British film industry, typified by the activities of J. Arthur Rank. Therefore a visit to the cinema became the nation's favourite form of entertainment and attendances reached their highest level, only declining in the late 1950s, after the end of rationing.

For those more familiar with the present-day experience of visiting a multiplex cinema, it may be interesting to recall the comparative wartime event. Firstly, most people would go to the Embassy, or other nearby cinema, at least once, probably twice and sometimes more frequently each week. Whilst a choice would usually be made as to which film to see, often it was the outing itself that was the motivation to obtain a break from the ambience of the War and its deprivations in exchange for a warm cosy cinema offering a few hours of escapism. This meant that with such a demand, most cinemas were full by mid-afternoon and long queues would form curling round the cinemas, with separate lines for each of the differently priced sections of seats! The main complexity was that most cinemas programmes comprised a main feature, second feature and the newsreel plus cartoons etc - operated on a continuous basis. The consequence was that because people were so anxious to get a seat they would enter at any point in the programme and stay for as long as they felt inclined. Certainly if they came in during a film they would stay to see it round again in order to understand the plot. Some would stay all day!

With the pressure to satisfy demand with ever more films, quality inevitably suffered. However, many classic films were made such as 'Casablanca' *and* 'A Matter of Life and Death'. *The latter was a product of the resurgent British film industry.* (CAF Coll.)

The result was that people were constantly being admitted from the queues outside to fill the places as others left. The management of the queues of potential customers was crucial and was usually in the hands of a commissionaire (large, burly and often an ex-serviceman) in an impressive uniform with gold piping. Needless to say, in effect, he 'policed' the cinema and delighted in wielding the power that he had over admitting the cold and tired individuals into the cinema. He would parade up and down the queues shouting out 'godlike' commands such as - "standing room only", "two single and a double 1/9's", the less desirable "two standing 2/-'s" because they would have to stand at the back of the stalls or circle waiting for seats to be vacated. Worst of all - "queuing all parts".

On entering, sometimes the Manager would be keeping an eye on sales. Indeed the long-serving Mr Smith often appeared in a dinner jacket. The tickets were paid for at a glass kiosk in the centre of the foyer and emerged in strips (of different colour according to price) from a chrome plate in the counter, the next step was to have it inspected by an usherette who tore it in half – returning one part and threading the other over a needle, on to a string for later checking.

There were two sets of doors to negotiate (to reduce spurious light and sound) to enter the actual auditorium. If there was an interval between films, then the lights would be on and whilst it was easier to attempt to find a seat, existing patrons were milling around, going to the toilets, looking for adjacent seats or better positions. However, usually one came in during a film and thus into what seemed to be utter darkness, whereupon an usherette would flash her torch in your face (to see what sort of person you were), then on your ticket and then vaguely to where there supposedly empty seats. Then the torch was extinguished and one was left to grope along a row of patrons until hopefully finding the seats. One's first sight was of the moving pictures on the screen, of normal shape if luckily one had a central seat, but badly distorted the further you had been placed to the side of the cinema (surprisingly, the eye and brain quickly adapted and converted it into the expected shape). In those days when smoking was the norm, the light from the projector room at the back of the circle cut a beam through the fug onto the screen. The screen formed a filter for the air conditioning and thus had to be regularly cleaned! However, soon one became absorbed in the picture until another interval and again people changing seats, getting ice creams from an usherette – or passing orders along the row!

As mentioned earlier, then there would often be a discussion as whether to leave having seen the all films, albeit in disjointed pieces, or stay in a comfortable seat-the latter usually won. For several years after the end of the War, the performance always ended with a patriotic film clip accompanied by the National Anthem. The lights would go up and the audience file out into the reality of Chesham.

The Embassy, like many other cinemas, also arranged special shows for children on Saturday mornings. These were welcomed by parents as getting the children out of the way. But Dave James, one of those children, recalls their first visit. *"I caught a bus down to the Embassy in Chesham, queued up, paid the sixpence to get in, found a seat amongst the noisy children, and settled down. It was plain to see that the children were there to enjoy themselves and the management let them get on with it - or were too nice to spoil their fun. I was amazed at the way the unruly mob behaved and sat there in disbelief at what I saw. I was used to going to the pictures and sitting very quietly in my seat without moving or larking about, but I soon found that Saturday morning pictures were very different. The children ran about everywhere, climbed over seats, had fights, yelled, and threw balls of paper and cartons at each other. Those with cycles were allowed to bring their cycle pumps in with them and they'd roll up a small ball of wet paper, stick into the end of their pump and 'shoot' it out with a quick stroke of the pump handle. These little balls of paper would sting viciously as they hit one's bare skin. Others not so fortunate as to have a cycle would bring an elastic band and, using two fingers as a prong, would make a small catapult to fire pieces of folded paper at their enemies. During the show we'd have one eye on the screen and one out for flying missiles. Sometimes even the people running the show would have to shut it down for a while*

A contemporary drawing that captures the excitement and chaos of the Saturday Chiltdren's Matinee. (Backnumbers)

until the noise quietened down. The manager would go up on the stage and tell us that he'd send us home if we didn't behave. The show would then re-start and all would be quiet until The Three Stooges, or something of that nature came on, then everyone would go mad again. After that would be a cartoon and a great cheer would go up as the familiar coloured rings would go up heralding a Bugs Bunny cartoon (see p36). They also used to show Roy Rodgers, Superman, Flash Gordon, Hopalong Cassidy and many other heroes of the day. The children would cheer like mad when these heroes would appear racing, at the last minute, to save the day. Apart from the cartoons, all the other films were in black and white. There was always an interesting documentary and a serial so that we'd come back next week to see if the hero got out of trouble, or not. After the show I'd come out into daylight pretending that I was the current hero, riding Trigger(Roy Rodger's horse) down the steps of the cinema and looking all ways in my search to take on all the crooks in Chesham."

THE ONSLAUGHT OF TELEVISION

After the war, with ongoing privations and a lack of competition in entertainment, the cinemas were still in their heyday. Under the long-serving manager, Mr Smith, queues stretched outside to see escapist films in a warm environment – even if in a smoke-laden atmosphere. He also encouraged the use of the cinema by local groups, like the Chesham Light Opera Company. However, by the 1950s things were changing with alternative leisure opportunities, competition from television and lacklustre films. The cinema industry fought back with CinemaScope, 3-D and

Twentieth-Century Fox re-introduced in 1953 an earlier invention of compressing a wide picture by means of a special lens on to conventional 35mm film. The resulting CinemaScope film 'The Robe' was a great success and led to a new generation of wide screen presentations from Panavision to IMAX. (Clive Foxell Collection)

Richard Wright, the new EMI Manager of the Embassy in 1980, with the latest projectors that had just been installed. Note the much greater size, mainly due to the powerful carbon arc light source, in comparison with the early machine shown on page 15. (Ray East Coll.)

Stereo sound but the inevitable decline resulted, with the Embassy being sold to EMI in 1980. The new manager, Richard Wright, installed new projectors etc, but the type of films on offer did not attract sufficient local people to sustain it, and even after strong protests and a petition, it closed in 1982. At that time, the Embassy still had some of the original staff, carpets and neon signs. The last film shown was *'Evil Under the Sun'* in April 1982 and the building was demolished (*as shown below*) in June 1983, being replaced by Townbridge Court retirement flats. If it had survived for longer there is little doubt that it would have been re-born as a 'multiplex' capable of showing films in the present popular mode of offering more choice of films, for longer periods, in smaller cinemas. In view of its iconic design some examples of the decorations are preserved in The Museum of London.

Demolition of the Embassy in progress during 1983: The view from stage looking towards the former circle and projection room can be compared with that on page 24.

Soon Townbridge Court, a development of retirement flats, was built on the site of the former Embassy Cinema. The road on the left passed through the original car park and Goodings Forge was just beyond the shop on the left. (Clive Foxell Photographs.)

BACK TO THE FUTURE

However, the cinema lived on in Chesham with the building of **The Elgiva** near the Library in 1976 *(below, top)*, as part of the re-development associated with the construction of St Mary's Way. With the closure of most cinemas in the district, the Chiltern Film Society used the Elgiva for their shows and this encouraged the installation of basic professional projection equipment leading to regular screening of mainstream films. Another redevelopment of this site as part of the arrival of Sainsbury's supermarket in 1998 included the demolition of the original Elgiva and the subsidised building of **The Second Elgiva** *(below, bottom)* as a *quid pro quo* for Council permission to redevelop the site beside St Mary's Way. With better facilities, including the latest Dolby sound and projection equipment, it has offered an eclectic choice of films. *(CAF Photos)*

Left: The projection room of the New Elgiva, showing by comparison with the pictures of earlier projectors, the ever-increasing length of the film spools and the reduction in the size of the light source due to new halogen and similar high performance lamps. (C A F Photo.)
Right: 'Titanic' was shown at both the old and new Elgiva's and the film represented the latest trend in production techniques, being shot with digital electronic video cameras and with much of the impressive special effects being created (as above) by Computer Generated Images. (Clive Foxell Collection)

Nevertheless, the cinema continues to evolve and now many productions are shot electronically in digital format using new high definition video techniques, which now at least equals the picture quality obtained by traditional film processes. This approach has several advantages. Firstly the cameraman and the director can watch the actual image being 'filmed' on video monitors, rather than through a viewfinder. Secondly, as the recording can be easily duplicated electronically, it potentially avoids the major cost of making hundreds of expensive film copies for distribution to cinemas. So the time is approaching when the programme can be downloaded over the telephone line (probably optical fibre) directly to The Elgiva, or its successor, to be shown by an electronic digital projector. The inherently lower cost of electronic distribution has wider implications in that it becomes economical to address smaller audiences with more specialised programmes such as opera, theatre, concerts or sport – let alone films!

The trend to digital technology is also facilitating the renewed attempt to introduce 3-D films, which had failed in the past due to complexities of filming with two cameras, then using two projectors and lastly the inconvenience of the audience having to view through special glasses. The current massive thrust to solve these problems has come from James Cameron (responsible for *Titanic*) making the first major 3-D film, *Avatar*. Improved Polaroid glasses are now available and electronically controlled versions are on trial.

Developments in Computer Generated Imaging are also making big advances; the realism of cartoons, like those by Pixar, is outstanding. Indeed it has been used to replace unavailable actors in conventional films!

But most of these developments are equally applicable to television in the home i.e large screens, high definition and 3-D, and so the basic question remains as to whether people will continue to prefer to watch outstanding programmes in the ambience of a cinema rather than on a TV at home. Nevertheless, the cinema has managed just to survive the massive onslaught of television and the availability of films on recording media from VHS to the latest disc technologies. At the peak of cinema popularity in 1950, there were some 4,800 (single screen) cinemas in the UK with attendances of about 27m people each week, paying an average of 1/6 for their tickets and generating an annual revenue of £1.35bn. By 1982 attendances had fallen to a low some 64m in the year, but the subsequent improvement in the quality of films and presentation has increased the current level to 175m. This reflects a decrease in number of cinemas to only about 775, but with the growth of multiplexes, films are being shown on about 3,660 screens generating annual revenues of £1bn.

Finally, just a cautionary footnote to the juggernaut of electronic progress. Currently, printing and film are the most practical means of making relatively permanent records, whereas electronic records depend on software and magnetic/optical memories – both of doubtful permanence! For example, it is now impossible to look at the original video recordings of the Moon Landing. So film may still have a role.

(Warner Bros.)

REFERENCES

The Bucks Examiner	Relevant Issues
Cinema statistics	The Cinema Exhibitors Association 2010
Clive Foxell	The (Ten!) Cinemas of Chesham Chess Valley Archaeological & Historical Society Journal 2007
Dave James	Chesham Memories -- members.inet.net.aul-dcjames 1997
Brian Coe	The History of Movie Photography Ash & Grant 1981
Patrick Robertson	Film Facts & Feats Guinness Superlatives 1980
Kevin Scrivens & Stephen Smith	The Travelling Cinematograph Show New Era Publications 1999
Martin Tapsell	Memories of Buckinghamshire Picture Palaces Mercia Cinema Society
National Fairground Archive	Bioscope Presenters: Alf Ball University of Sheffield

APPENDICES

How to Change Over Projectors

As mentioned earlier, during the heyday of the cinema, the length of feature films had increased to the extent that they were carried on several spools. Consequently, two projectors were required to provide a continuous performance and, in order to give a seamless show, the operator had to carry out faultlessly an extremely complex series of operations to change projectors and yet still retain continuity of the pictures and sound. Below are the typical instructions for the projectionists at The Embassy Cinema.

'When about a ½ in. layer of film is left on the upper spool of the first projector (No.1) currently showing the film, this leaves about one minute of running time before the changeover. The projectionist should then take up a position between the two projectors, in such a manner that the left hand is on the switches for projector No.1, and the switches of machine No.2 can be operated by the right hand. In this position the projected picture must watched through the observation port. When the finish of the current spool is imminent, a small mark will appear, usually in the top right of the picture, about 8½ seconds before the end, and with the right hand turn the motor of machine No.2 'On'. Immediately thereafter, put the right hand on the lamp switch. Place the left hand on the lamp switch of projector No. 1 and seven seconds after the first cue the second changeover cue will appear. At that moment, simultaneously throw the lamp switch of machine No.2 'On' and the lamp switch of machine No. 1 'Off' - and continue with the left hand to the amplifier controls and throw the changeover switch to the right to '2'. Be instantly ready to turn the amplifier volume control up or down and frame the picture in the event either is necessary. As soon as the film in projector No.1 has run out, stop the machine and thread it with the next reel.

The footage number to be threaded in the gate aperture depends on the characteristics of the individual projector i.e. acceleration of the motor and thus has to be found by experiment. Standard exchange prints all have the leader at the beginning of the reel with indicators marked on each film frame, beginning 'start' and then with the numbers 11 to 3. The threading number should be adjusted until a perfect changeover is made and the value noted on the threading diagram on the inside of the projector door for the benefit of other operators.'

To see this sequence in action was impressive and it was performed many thousands of times without the audience aware of the skills of the projectionist.